FROM BLACKHEATH TO GOODWOOD

JOHN SWIFT

FROM BLACKHEATH TO GOODWOOD

Copyright © 2025 by John Swift
All rights reserved. No part of this book may be reproduced in any manner whatsoever without written permission except in the case of brief quotations embodied in critical articles and reviews.
First Printing, 2025

CONTENTS

Foreword
vii

— The Stories
1

1 — The Neighbours
2

2 — The First Cut is the Deepest
9

3 — Big Yellow Taxi
12

4 — What's on the Menu?
16

5 — The Visitors
20

6 — Everyday Stuff
25

7 — Sundays
30

8 — HQ Blackheath
35

9 – War Games and Tunnels
39

10 – Unexpected
44

11 – Farm Life
51

– Photo Insert
0

– Photo Insert
0

– Photo Insert
0

– Photo Insert
0

– Photo Insert
0

12 – School Holidays
62

– Photo Insert
0

13 – Primary School Days
69

14 – The High School Years (1963 - 1965)
74

– Additional Reflections
82

15 – Health Matters
83

16 — Two or Three a Penny?
91

17 — Final Words
94

FOREWORD

In the stories that follow I have tried, somewhat successfully I hope, not to be guilty of stretching the truth, but rather to recall to the best of my ability some of the more interesting memories of my younger years during the 1950s and early 60s with the hope of not only entertaining you the reader, but of also painting a picture of what it was like for a young boy to grow up in institutional care and therefore without the support of parents and the security of the family home.

Although I have endeavoured to arrange the stories in a chronological order, as much as they will allow, they were originally written to stand alone, each one dealing with specific topics to highlight events that took place during my early years. That is how they are to be read, as individual stories which together form a whole and give the reader a clearer understanding of what life was like.

The telling of them is not for the purpose of seeking the reader's sympathy — though maybe some empathy will help the reader to understand the stories more fully. My own reflections regarding those early years have helped me to come to the conclusion that though they were sometimes difficult, these years were full of life's lessons which have helped me to live a full life, and for that at least, I am grateful for God's good providence.

This 'book' may never have been written except for the persistent encouragement of my wife Beverley, who over the years has insisted that our children and now grandchildren as well as others would find it interesting to read about my rather different early childhood experiences. I now thank her for her persistence and encouragement in helping me to complete the stories.

I am grateful also to Rodney, my younger brother with whom I spent the years at Blackheath and later at Goodwood. Rod's presence during those years was for me a constant reminder that we had a mum and extended family outside the places where we were growing up and that at least gave one a sense of belonging which was a good feeling. I also felt a sense of responsibility because being the older brother mum had made me promise to look after Rod, something I was determined to do.

In the writing of these stories, Rod has been of valuable assistance in helping me to recall some of the finer details, and in particular what those years were like for him. Being almost three years younger than myself, he has very little recollection of life before Blackheath.

The experience we shared together formed a bond between us that enables us now as elderly men to reflect and sometimes to ponder the question — what if life's circumstances had been different?

Most of all, I hope that these stories will help you the reader to come to a better understanding of what life in institutional care was like for thousands of young Australians growing up in the years after the second world war.

John E Swift

THE STORIES

THE NEIGHBOURS

"Neighbours, everybody needs good neighbours" - so the television drama song goes. Life has taught me that there's some truth contained in this little jingle. An old bishop once told a small gathering I attended that the world was reverting to tribalism and that ideally we humans liked to hangout in packs of eight. Looking back over my life I would agree that much of it has been spent in small groups. My earliest years for example were spent living at Shaw Road, Wavell Heights surrounded by good neighbours.

Over the lower side of our back fence lived the Thompson family and one up from them, the Hutchinsons. Across the road on a large triangular block lived the Riley family. On the other side of Shaw Road were the Hopsicks and next door on the upper side lived the Geddes family who became our close friends. So, we were surrounded with friendly families who had children, which meant lots of friends to play with. We were often to be found at one or other's homes.

In the 1950s small metal matchbox cars were very popular and a favourite past time was to be underneath a house making roads in the dirt with our hands to drive our cars on. Sometimes, when a small group of us got together we would dress up and play cowboys and indians armed with our cap guns, bows and arrows. Some of us wore Davey Crockett caps and if we owned them, cowboy pants with holsters for our six-guns, the indians wore a head band with feathers stuck in it and maybe some war paint (lip stick or white cream) on the face. On one occasion I ended up in serious trouble with my father for shooting my younger brother just below his eye with an arrow. No harm was done in the long term, but in the short term I had a very sore behind from Dad's razor strop.

I was drawn to the new Hutchinson boy as soon as he arrived on the scene. He had come from Port Moresby in New Guinea where I believe his father had held a public servant position. Jimmy brought a number of artefacts with him including a native war drum that we all enjoyed beating and trying to make it sound as Jimmy said it should, but with little success. I remember not long after his arrival going with him and his Dad to collect their new English bulldog pup - Frosty. The young pup was as white as snow with some small black markings on his face. How cuddly he first appeared, but he grew up to become a fearsome looking beast with a deep growl who didn't like most visitors to their house - especially the postman.

Across the street the Riley home was a large white weatherboard Queenslander and I recall Mrs Riley as always being warm and hospitable toward the local children. She had a large family, and was always cleaning up around the house or in the kitchen cooking. Her youngest son Michael and his sister Denise became great friends and I remember Michael allowing me to have a ride, my first ever, on his new bike. I did okay, but then, the training wheels were still attached! Many years later when I called in to visit Mrs Riley she recalled how terrified I was of her old Hoover vacuum cleaner. "As soon as I would switch on the power and the Hoover started making its loud sucking sound, you would yell out 'Mrs Riley I have to go home now' and you'd be gone in a flash." We both had a bit of a chuckle.

Michael had a much older brother, John I think, and he was always in the backyard tinkering with his old car. Sometimes if we became a bit of a nuisance by hanging around and asking too many questions, especially when his girlfriend was there, he would tell us to scram. I was always a bit unsure about him and never knew what to expect if he started to become annoyed, especially when we were running around his car playing tiggy or hiding in the old wooden garage playing hide and seek.

Just over the street from the Riley home on the corner of Shaw Rd lived a very interesting man who owned a horse and buggy. Sometimes when the rig was set up he would offer the local boys and girls a ride around the neighbourhood. We loved climbing up on the seat and hanging on while the horse trotted off down the street. Everybody enjoyed these rides immensely.

This old man, every adult seemed old to me then, is also remembered because on Guy Fawkes night, he would have the biggest bonfire and Guy in our neighbourhood. Families from all around the area would would come to watch and bring their fire crackers including some sky rockets which were awesome to watch as they zoomed into the night sky. I don't think anyone knew where they landed but an enjoyable and memorable night was had by all.

The Hopsicks lived opposite on the other side of Shaw Road. Because of the road I was rarely at their house but I do vividly recall one incident that took place at the low set brick house next-door to theirs. We had been playing hide and seek when someone decided it would be a good trick to lock the door to underneath the house where I was hiding. I had left the door slightly ajar when I went under the house because there were quite a few cobwebs and it was quite dark under there. Suddenly it slammed shut. I could hear them laughing on the other side of the door. I tried not to let them know how frightened I was, locked under there for what seemed to me to be quite some time in the dark. Suddenly I heard an adult's voice outside and then the door was opened. I crawled out into the bright sunshine and immediately bolted for home!

When I was two years old a newly married couple, Heather and Warring Geddes moved into the house next door on the upper side. My mother Phyllis and Heather became close friends until Mum died in her mid-forties. She had been in poor health for many years by then but through it all Heather remained her close friend. Often they would have lunch together at Heather's and then enjoy playing the pianola together, and chatting into the afternoon. When Mum was ill and in hospital, Heather and Warring visited her when very few others including her own extended family didn't. Heather became my Godmother at my baptism, and I grew up calling her Aunty Heather. Of course that meant that Warring became Uncle Warring.

By the time I was about four years old, it seemed like all the children wanted to spend their time playing at Aunty Heather's home. We all loved her and the attention she gave us. What I liked most was helping her in the kitchen with an unusual device she called the mincer which she clamped to the edge of the tabletop. Under Heather's guidance we cut large slices of steak into smaller pieces and usually one child would feed these into the opening at the top of the mincer while another turned the handle on the side and after a few turns, presto! Out of the side of the mincer came the newly processed mince steak which was collected on a tray positioned to receive it. Another kitchen appliance I will always identify with Heather's kitchen was her pressure cooker. It was always whistling away on her stove as the steam escaped. I was initially quite captivated by it as my mum didn't have one.

From left - John, Rod with Neil and Robert (neighbours)

If one of her boys was having a birthday party, Aunty Heather's was the place to be. There would be lots of cordial and cakes of various kinds followed by games like 'pass the parcel' and 'pin the tail on the donkey' and others that we all enjoyed very much. We all went home with a bag of sweets and maybe a balloon.

These days it seems everybody has a mobile phone in their pocket but rarely use them to actually speak to other people directly, teenagers especially. Instead, texting is all the rage. I find this rather amusing since the original telephone invented by Alexander Graham Bell was considered a modern day wonder when for the first time two people could actually speak to one another over long distances replacing the older invention of Morse Code, a series of dots and dashes sent over telegraph wires and decoded at the other end. To my mind, it was an early form of texting, the message was sent and received without a word spoken.

That's why, when the Geddes' household installed a telephone all the neighbourhood kids wanted to see it. I remember it being rather heavy, made of black bakelite with a large silver metal dial with which the phone numbers were dialled, and a large heavy receiver that the operator held up to the ear and mouth to listen and speak. Everyone wanted a turn to make a call and or listen in, but because calls were expensive we were not permitted to touch it.

Heather took her role as my Godmother quite seriously, and after mum became ill she and Warring took me to live with them for a while. In later years my brother Rodney and I stayed a number of times at their home during the end of the year Christmas holidays. These holiday stays did not always go without a hitch or two, such as the time when we were driven down to the Gold Coast to stay at Kirra Beach for week or so. On the drive down Heather noticed Rod was reading a comic book. She became quite angry with him because he was reading rubbish and not enjoying the lovely view as we drove down the highway.

On another occasion for some unknown reason, Rodney ran away. By the time Heather noticed he was gone, Rod was well on his way across town to stay with Mum and Grandad. Somehow he managed to find his way from Wavell Heights all the way to Hendra without being found. Everyone was in a fluster looking for him by then so on his arrival, the reception was not what he had been expecting. He was eventually picked up by Heather and Warring and driven back to Wavell Heights for the rest of our stay.

Recently Rod mentioned his reason for running away was simply that he was missing his Mum. The poor kid, he always seemed to be getting in trouble for just wanting to be like other kids who lived at home with their Mum and Dad.

So then, for the first five years or so of my life, as I recall it, I lived in a friendly neighbourhood with lots of friends to play with and not a care in the world for our safety. Circumstances were about to change. How that affected my life and that of my younger brother Rodney is the theme of the stories that make up the rest of this book.

THE FIRST CUT IS THE DEEPEST

My first home in Shaw Rd Wavell Heights

"Well, I never!" These were my first thoughts as I viewed the old house in Shaw Road, Wavell Heights. The roof was in need of attention, the paint was peeling off large sections of the weatherboards, the front fence was broken and the grass was very long. A feeling of sadness clouded over me as I took a photo of my childhood home for my first six years. I remembered it as a new freshly-painted home with neat lawns and an attractive front fence with gates to keep me from running onto the road, but never like this.

Memories of those years are still clear some seventy years later. Some have said I was the apple of my father's eye during those years and I remember distinctly feeling the growing bond between us back then. My Dad served in the army during WWII as a radio mechanic and later as a radio mechanic for Chandlers. He drove a cream coloured Morris panel van with the famous HMV dog sitting in front of a gramophone horn painted on its side panel. Never was I happier than after school when Dad would take me with him to collect radios he repaired that night at home. Many times I fell asleep at the kitchen table watching him changing valves and repairing circuits with his soldering iron. Sometimes we would stop off on the way home for a swim at Cribb Island beach. Never since have I seen so many soldier crabs massed together and moving along the wet sand like a large blue blanket of cloud. Sometimes we would collect shell grit in a small hessian bag for the chook pen. Dad had given me two beautiful bantams, a small rooster I named Red, and Blackie a small black hen. Dad would sometimes gently hold Red's head so that it faced the ground and then draw a straight line in the dirt while releasing his hold. Red would just stand there mesmerised starring at the ground until we moved him. My young eyes found it incredibly entertaining.

Parents often are the primary influence for their young children and from around the age of five my two main interests were radios and aeroplanes. Dad made me a balsa wood plane with a propeller that would spin when held out of the car window. Sadly one day during a drive it detached itself - never to be seen again. I was devastated!

But, back to my then first love - radio. My favourite was a crystal set that Dad had made for me. It was fitted into a small cigar box with a jack on the side for plugging in the headphones. I really treasured it and enjoyed listening in.

Never was a boy happier to have a Dad like mine.

And never was a boy so traumatised, when late one night he left for good with not even a goodbye. During my early childhood he did this three times, once from Shaw Rd, once from the new house at Geebung and once from his mother's home.

But the first time cut deep into my soul and left a scar that time has not fully healed.

CHAPTER 3

BIG YELLOW TAXI

During the late 1950's Yellow Cabs provided a popular means of travel in Brisbane. Their yellow FJ Holden taxis were a common sight across the city. It was a journey in one of these taxis that was to instil memories that my younger brother and I, aged six and four years at the time, still discuss more than sixty-five years later.

At the time, we had been staying with our father and his mother, grandma Swift, at her home. One evening, after we had been bathed and put to bed and told to go to sleep, I overheard the end of a conversation between them. "Poor little buggers!" I heard him say and then all was quiet.

I didn't know it at the time but they were probably the last words I heard from my father for the next fifty years when I briefly made contact with him.

The next morning - he was gone!

Many years later, the song "Big Yellow Taxi" sung by Joni Mitchell appeared on the pop charts with lyrics that still tug at my heart strings, though not as forcefully as in former years.

Late last night / I heard the screen door slam /
And a big yellow taxi / Took away my old man.
"Don't it always seem to go /
That you don't know what you got 'til it's gone?"

After breakfast, Grandma had both of us neatly dressed, when a bright FJ Holden yellow taxi pulled up outside the front door. We were quickly bundled into the rear seat and after she had given instructions to the driver, we were on our way across Brisbane. What was happening, where were we going?

It was, I thought, like a big adventure. We had no idea where the driver was taking us, but we enjoyed travelling in his car and holding on to the silver hand rail that was across the back of the front bench seat.

Then suddenly the car slowed. "Here we are boys!" He said pointing to the house as he stopped outside. "That's Pop's house!" my younger brother Rod said excitedly. Our mum, who had been in hospital had recently gone to stay with her father, so we were excited to see her come out of the house towards the car.

Suddenly, Grandad, also known to us as Pop, stormed across the yard to the driver and demanded to know what was going on.

The driver, taken by surprise by this, explained that he had been asked to deliver us two boys to this address and that was that. Pop however, was not having that! He was a big tall man of German descent who could be quite intimidating and liked to flout his authority when it came to family matters. And, he had very little time for our short, slim and widowed English grandmother.

I think he was jealous of her because she was financially independent and owned her own home while he rented his.

Anyhow, it wasn't long before, against our mother's pleas of "no dad, please, let them stay" that we were again heading off in the yellow taxi, back the way we came. On arrival, the driver went in to speak with our grandmother. Only a few minutes later we were off again, this time with an agitated driver who explained along the way that if he could not drop us off this time, he was sorry, but he would have to take us to the police station because he didn't know what else to do.

With all that had taken place, we had started to become frightened and confused as to why we couldn't stay with our mum and grandad. It had dawned on us that nobody seemed to want us. Had we done something wrong to end up at the police station? It would be some years yet before we would come to fully understand the meaning of rejection, but we certainly both felt emotionally about what it meant, firstly as young children that day and later on into adolescence and adulthood.

The police took us both, aged four and six years, into custody and I think a very relieved yellow taxi driver drove off having certainly earned his fare for that day.

"We are going to have some lunch; you boys must be hungry. Would you like some too?" asked the police sergeant's wife. She served up a delicious ham and salad lunch that we washed down with cold cordial.

That was to be our last home made meal for some years, the following morning it would be rolled oats complete with weevils on rusty tin plates.

"Okay then, off we go," said the sergeant and we were ushered into the police car for another trip across town.

After a long drive, we arrived at what might have been in earlier times, a huge old-fashioned, multi-storied guest house surrounded by enormous grounds with a very long driveway leading up to the front of the building. The house had a wide verandah on two sides with steps leading up to the front door. On arrival we were met by a serious looking overweight older woman wearing a grey dress, and whom I can't ever remember smiling in the years I knew her.

We would learn that she was the matron of the Blackheath Boys Home at Oxley, and the first thing she said to us was - "boys, each of you take a rug from the pile over there, find a spot on the floor, keep quiet and go to sleep."

I looked up at her just for the briefest moment, then took a rug and lay down on the floor.

Lying there that afternoon, and for many years after while in the care of the Presbyterian Church, one constant thought was uppermost in my mind -

"I want to go home!"

CHAPTER 4

WHAT'S ON THE MENU?

The dining room was huge with the tables and chairs set up in a u-shape for the sixty plus boys, and another smaller table set apart like the bridal table at a wedding or the head table for the principal and staff at a college. Matron Adamson sat at the centre of this table with her husband and son on one side and members of staff on the other. From her central position she could observe all of us boys as we ate our meals - or not.

Each morning we were served rolled oats with a little milk on brown coloured tin plates which often contained surface rust that had accumulated over night due to them being stacked while still wet. The oats usually arrived at the kitchen in large hessian bags and were usually infested with weevils. So, when the porridge was served up, it did not look like the most appealing meal with which to start the day.

Except for the rather bland taste, there was nothing wrong with rolled oats for breakfast, it was just those damn weevils that everyone hated and a considerable amount of time was spent trying to pick them out.

What really got up our noses though, was the fact that our menu was totally different to that served up at the head table. Matron and those seated at her table would usually start with a bowl, china not tin, of Kellogg's Rice Bubbles with warm milk and sugar. This was followed by bacon and eggs, toast and marmalade with a cup of tea. Many was the time I was green with envy and wished I could eat at that table as I watched the matron's son holding up a bacon rash dipped in egg with his fingers to feed his German Shepherd dog.

I have a sneaky feeling that matron A knew just how much we envied the meals served on her table because she came up with an idea that helped to get the boys to empty their plates more quickly. She would eat about half of her rice bubbles, then look around the dining room for a boy who had eaten all his oats and was sitting up straight. She would then call out this boy by name and his reward was to be given her remaining rice bubbles to eat. Her idea worked like a treat and created quite a bit of competition amongst the boys including myself, a lucky recipient on a number of occasions. Oh, how I enjoyed those rice bubbles in the sugary warm milk, though when I think about it now, scenes from Oliver Twist always flash through my mind and I wonder what the result might have been if, on one of the occasions when I was the fortunate one to have had my name called out, I had stood, bowl in hand and asked, "please matron could I have some more?" Words like ungrateful wretch come to mind!

The Sunday lunchtime meal, served after the boys had changed out of their Sunday best clothes, was a cooked meal and sometimes it was corned beef, cabbage and mashed potato. On one such occasion, after we had completed the meal and those on kitchen duties were in the process of cleaning up, matron A appeared just as we were about to scrape a couple of plates containing fat and gristle into the pig bin. She ordered us to stop what we were doing and gave an order to recall all the boys to the dining room. When this was done the plates containing the leftovers were brought in and after a few words about 'waste not want not' we were each given a piece of the leftovers to eat. My brother who still won't eat fatty meat especially corned beef to this day, assures me that he and some others stuffed their piece of fat into their pant's pocket while others managed to drop it through a nearby window.

Evening meals were interesting because their preparation could give hints as to who might be coming to dinner. We were often served a kind of baked stew, a mixture of vegetables, chops and sausage in a thick gravy. This was cooked in large rectangular metal trays and if somebody of importance was visiting for the mealtime a pastry crust was added across the top but I noted, not otherwise. I liked the pastry topping, but it meant you had to be careful when eating what was hidden under it, like bits of sharp chop bone. I have often wondered if the pastry topping was added purely to dress up what was otherwise a fairly average looking meal, though I must admit that apart from the bits of bone I enjoyed the stew.

Sometimes we felt the need to supplement the dining room meals with whatever we could find growing in the vicinity. Depending on the season we enjoyed helping ourselves to the cherry tomatoes that grew wild along the edges of the rubbish tip out the back of the kitchen as well as mangoes, persimmons and mulberries that grew on trees in properties along the roads to the school and railway station. Of course we had to leave the grounds to obtain these fruits so the trick was not to get caught.

One of the things I feared most and that I later learned was the result of being fed a diet that was low in nutrition, and not from eating mangoes, was boils. When you were unlucky enough to get them, and many of us boys did, the pain could be excruciating. One of my most painful experiences was to have several of these at the same time, one of which was on my backside and prevented me from sitting down. For three days at school I had to stand at the back of the class because of the pain when sitting. The only thing worse than the pain of the boil was the treatment which required the patient to expose the boil so that wax melted by a flame could be dripped onto it. In my case this meant being held over a dining room chair while the deed was done. I have never forgotten the experience and still wear the scar to remind me.

So, what's on the menu? I don't know but I hope it's served on clean china plates, is low in fat, contains no bone chips, rust or weevils and that it's tastier and more nutritious than were those served up at the Blackheath Boys Home!

CHAPTER 5

THE VISITORS

A visit from a family member could often add some zest to the routine of institutional life at Blackheath. These usually took place on Saturdays and for those reliant on public transport, it meant a journey by train to Oxley station followed by a ten minute walk up a slight hill to the property. Because we were not allowed out of the property several of the boys, myself included, would climb a very large tree on the grounds that had long thick branches extending out horizontally from the main trunk. We had to be on alert because both being found off the property and climbing trees were both punishable with the strap across one's backside.

From our high position in the tree and looking like birds on a wire, we could see anyone walking up the road toward us. I remember how excited we were perched up there trying to identify prospective visitors. But it wasn't just the family members we were looking for, we were waiting and hoping for someone who would be carrying a parcel containing treats and maybe a comic or two. After the visitors had gone we often traded these things and sometimes a little bit of money we had been given - never declared to the staff, for other items like comics, marbles, plastic soldiers, knuckle bones and collectors cards.

There were many Saturday afternoons we spent perched in that old tree waiting and watching to no avail. I felt so disappointed when it happened week after week.

Most of our visits were from uncle Bert, our mum's brother and he always brought us a 'little something'. Later in life, I came to understand how difficult it must have been for him without a car as he often visited mum who was in hospital further along the railway line before coming to see us on the return journey. He was employed in a large retail store in the city and in those days was required to work until twelve noon on Saturdays. A lifelong bachelor, he spent his life looking after his mother and father as well as our mum and us two boys. I still have a couple of greeting cards he sent us in the mail. We were fortunate that nobody opened them before we did as they came bearing gifts inside, usually a ten shilling note which was a small fortune in our eyes. Although the demon drink got a grip on him in later years, I will always be grateful to him for the kindness he showed us.

Occasionally there were visits to Blackheath by others like the members of APEX. We dreaded these visits because it meant it was haircuts for us on the large verandah. If you have ever had your hair cut by untrained men using manual clippers then you will understand why we were loathe to come forward when we heard the call - "NEXT!"

I remember well the clippers catching and sometimes pulling out bits of hair that the barber hadn't planned to remove. Ouch! was a word heard a lot as well as a few other expletives on occasion that shouldn't have been said by boys of any age. These were no stylists cutting our hair, and the result was often short back and sides with uneven edges.

At the other end of the verandah there was another man set up with a small table and a stool. On the table was a large tin and a dish cloth. When the barber was finished with us, we were required to sit on this stool and the man would dip his cloth into the kerosene in the tin and give us a good dousing with it. I hated the feeling of the kerosene running down my neck while trying to keep my eyes shut because once it got in, it stung like crazy. I believe this procedure was to rid us of any head lice we might be carrying in our hair. I don't know how successful it was, but I am grateful to still have a full head of hair sixty-five years later!

Then, there was the worst feared visitor of all, the travelling dentist!

He too would set himself up on the large wide verandah with quite a strange contraption, part of which looked like the back end of a push bike. It was connected to dentistry equipment and a drill.

"Hop up into the chair young fella and we will have a look at your teeth."

After my first experience of him 'looking at my teeth,' I left the chair in agony, having received a large filling in one of my front teeth. It was a time before narrow bore anaesthetic injections and the speed of the drill depended on how fast the bike was peddled! I remained terrified of dentists for most of my life following that experience, and recently shared it with the young female dentist I now visit after she asked "why are you so tense?"

"Oh, wow," she exclaimed after I explained, "we saw one of those machines in the museum when I was training! I never thought I would meet anyone who had actually been treated with one - oh wow, you poor thing!"

But, there were happier times, all was not doom and gloom. Guy Fawkes night also known as cracker night was always a time to look forward to. Though it was later banned in 1972 in Queensland because of the injuries people suffered, we loved it. The scouts would meet with us on the large oval and build a huge bonfire with a guy stuffed with straw on the top. An old wire bed base was mounted over another smaller prepared campfire and this served as a barbecue on which the scouts cooked a heap of sausages. Wrapped in a slice of bread, we consumed them as fast as they could cook them. It seemed to me that even the smell around the barbecue was delicious.

Then when it became completely dark, the bonfire was lit and there was a fireworks display that always got my full attention. I loved watching the sky rockets shooting up into the night sky, the Roman Candles and the sound of strings of Tom Thumbs going off as well as the explosions all over the oval of the larger crackers. The many sparklers also made a dazzling display as they were waved around in the night air.

To conclude this fun time we sat around the bonfire, some eating marshmallows cooked on wires held over the coals and sang songs that the scouts taught us, songs like "There's a hole in the bucket dear Liza", "My eyes are dim I cannot see, I have not brought my specks with me", "Ten green bottles sitting on the wall" and others. Guy Fawkes night really was a fun time and could be profitable too, for if we were lucky we could usually find a few unexploded fireworks that we could use as ammo when playing war games down in the scrub.

Another of my favourite visitors apart from uncle B and mum on the few occasions she could come to see us, was the man from The Band Of Hope Temperance League. He would be set up in the main dining room and usually brought with him a couple of short movies that he screened from a rather noisy reel to reel movie projector which sometimes broke down. He usually ran a cartoon and then another movie that taught something about the evils of alcohol. After the movies he would ask us questions about what we had seen and there would be small rewards for those who had listened carefully and gave good answers. Sometimes he would bring a small crate of soft drinks and other goodies as prizes. On one such occasion just before the end of year school holidays we were asked to write down on bits of paper he supplied what we wanted for Christmas.

Little devil that I was, with my eyes fixed firmly on the soft drinks wrote, " I want to spend Christmas with my mum and go to church with her on Christmas Day."

Sure enough I won the first prize, which consisted of a packet of lollies and a soft drink.

Later, I had mixed emotions about my win though. I have always had a sensitive conscience and somehow I felt that God was watching me and perhaps was not happy about what I had written, especially after reciting out loud the Band of Hope pledge earlier. - "I promise God helping me to abstain from all intoxicating liquor and to get others to do the same."

I wasn't really sure what intoxicating liquor was, where you purchased it or for that matter how to abstain from it, let alone how to get other people to do the same. But I had been taught by my Sunday School teacher that God watches over us for our good and I thought that if God was against it, then it must be bad.

And so the weeks turned into months and years, and the visitors came and went and life at Blackheath continued on.

EVERYDAY STUFF

Keeping the Blackheath property running efficiently was achieved through a combined effort of staff members and resident boys who were assigned various tasks using a roster system. These included cleaning and maintaining the grounds and internal duties like preparing the meals, dining room and cleaning up afterwards as well as removing bedding and dirty clothes to the laundry and putting out the garbage.

Children living in the average suburban family home are it's true, often required to complete chores, the more fortunate for pocket money. But Blackheath was different in that the number and size of the chores was much larger due to the number of people and the property size, and there was definitely no pocket money to be had except for the matron's son who I learned, was successful in getting his parents to pay him to attend school.

I remember being on the roster to rake the leaves off the front lawns. This could be a horrible job especially in the winter months when the westerly winds were blowing and I could be out there freezing for an hour or more. On other occasions I found myself on kitchen duty over the large double sink with another boy washing and peeling potatoes, more than sixty of them for the next evening meal. Another regular duty was making the school lunches. I cannot remember how many slices of bread I buttered but it was a lot and seemed to go on forever. After the spread, usually vegemite or peanut paste had been added, the sandwiches were wrapped in square sheets of plastic that the boys returned each afternoon to be washed and reused the next day. They were only replaced when the plastic became hard and yellowed and began to crack or tear.

Institutions can be difficult places in which to survive, and I remember how the older boys as a rule managed to end up with the lunches wrapped in the new plastic wrappers and the smaller younger boys got what was left. There is no doubt in my mind that it helped to have a mate on duty when queuing for items.

Kids can be cruel, and at school the home boys and their lunches were sometimes picked on by other students because of their appearance. One instance took place during the end of year breakup. Our class teacher had us all combine our lunches by placing them on a picnic table from which we could all share the food. Though she meant well, and I was excited about getting my hands on some of the cupcakes on display, the whole exercise became very embarrassing when none of the children would eat any of the sandwiches that came from the boys home. "Don't touch that, that's home boy food!" I heard one boy say with a smirk on his face to a couple of his mates. Though the teacher was quick to give him a dressing down, the damage had been done, I saw the looks on some of the faces of children near me and I wished that I could run away or become invisible.

One of the best inventions of the modern era in my experience has been the dishwasher. It's a crying shame that we didn't have one. Following meal times we stacked and returned the dirty plates, cups and cutlery back to the kitchen for those unlucky enough to find themselves on the washing up detail. You either washed, dried or stacked the items in their respective shelves. But before the washing up could begin, the scraps had to be scrapped into the 'pig bin'. Quite often I would be one of two who had the job of carrying the bin full of scraps down the back of the house to the pig pen. The carrying was done by placing a long pole through the bin handle and then lifting it up onto our shoulders. We normally managed okay except for the one obstacle along the way. The pig pen was enclosed within a much larger fenced area that contained a rather nasty billy goat that seemed to delight in attempting to charge at anyone walking across his territory. More than once we had to drop the pig bin and run for our lives! That goat was definitely not my best mate!

Somehow, we always managed to outsmart him and deliver the scraps into the pig trough and we thought that was a job well done.

Located on the upper floor of the house were the dormitories where we were each assigned a bed. Rod and I slept on the long enclosed verandah that must have contained at least twenty five painted galvanised iron beds with another half dozen or so cots running across the end of these. When we first arrived Rod slept in one of those cots. There was a strict rule that we were not to drink anything after six in the evening. This was I believe a measure that was taken to help prevent bed wetting but it was in my opinion a harsh way of dealing with an issue that only affected a few. Those who were unfortunate enough to wet the bed during the night were often held up to ridicule and or given some form of punishment to prevent them doing it again.

On laundry day we stripped the beds of sheets and pillowcases and some of us would remove them down to our laundryman

Yossie, an elderly thin Japanese man who ran the laundry all on his own. Looking back, I really don't know how he managed it. He was a very quiet and sensitive man, who rarely spoke to anyone and I only saw him in the laundry or shuffling along in his flip flops and Japanese smoking jacket to his room at the end of the verandah on which I slept. He always locked the door behind him when he went in and no sound was ever heard from his room. He seemed to me somehow mysterious and I was intrigued by him. Many years later Yossie came to my mind when I was listening to a Simon and Garfunkel song, "A Most Peculiar Man" from their popular album Sounds of Silence. On reflection, he was Japanese and it was Brisbane in the early post war years and maybe that explains his quietly withdrawn demeanour. I will never know.

What I do know is that somehow he washed and ironed our dirty school uniforms and always had them ready to be reissued when required.

The clothes were placed on a long table that had the top painted with squares containing numbers that corresponded to the number assigned to us when we arrived at Blackheath, I was thirty-six and Rod was thirty-five, never to be forgotten as was my much later RAAF service number.

Our numbers, 35 and 36, were used mainly for laying out the clothes we would be given to wear to school and on Sundays to church. Quite often you could end up with a shirt or shorts that didn't fit correctly and would have to wait till the next handout to maybe get something more suitable. This could be very embarrassing at school.

On one occasion I was rostered to hand out the school uniforms. When Rod arrived at the service desk, I was determined to give him something nice to wear that would fit him. "Thirty-five," he said and I went to get his clothes from the square numbered thirty-five. I noticed that the shorts and shirt were too big so I quickly swapped them for smaller sizes. When I returned and passed them through to him, I noticed his eyes light up and he smiled as he turned to go. But, as he walked back through the locker room he hadn't noticed that the matron was right behind him, he was still smitten with his good luck. "For once in my bloody life I've got something decent to wear!" he blurted out.

The next thing he knew someone had him by his hair. "You ungrateful little so and so!" she yelled at him, and still holding him by the hair, she dragged him all the way to her office where Rod tells me she "well and truly got stuck into me with the strap, and when she was finished made me stand in the corner facing the wall for ages until I could hardly stand any longer."

To misquote Ned Kelly slightly - such was life. And it was, but a future generation would judge it not only as inappropriate, but harsh, even cruel and worthy of an apology and financial compensation.

CHAPTER 7

SUNDAYS

He was tall and walked with his shoulders back, his head erect and a jockey whip tucked under his left armpit as would an army officer carrying his swagger stick. His hair was reddish brown and never seemed to change in length or style which led some of us to conclude that Mr Adamson wore a toupee, something we young boys thought was hilarious. He was not as conspicuous around the house and grounds as was Mrs Adamson, the matron, but Mr A had the uncanny knack of turning up when we were about our chores or preparing to leave for school or church on Sundays.

Whenever we left the grounds, he gave the order to 'fall in' in ranks of three with the tallest boys to the front and rear of the squad and the shorter and younger ones in the middle. This was followed by the order to 'right dress' to achieve straight lines, then while standing to attention we heard among other things about the importance of keeping in step when we marched off. One could have been forgiven for thinking we were in the army and not a group of boys going to school or church.

Preparation for Sunday's train journey from Oxley to Central in the city began on Saturday when as a group we got out the Kiwi black nugget shoe polish and brushes. Mr A would usually make an appearance and spur us on with his usual comment, "Make sure the toes are shiny now, and also the heels. You can always tell the cut of a man by the shine on his shoes!" I wonder what he would say about the youth of today, many of whom have never put nugget to leather!

Sunday was special, it was the day we wore our best clothes which consisted of white shirts, grey knickerbocker shorts worn with long socks and our polished black shoes. In cooler months we wore a v-necked maroon jumper. We must have looked a sight marching down to Oxley railway station and then Ann St past the Salvation Army Band playing hymns, to Ann Street Presbyterian Church.

Sunday was also exciting because of the enjoyable return train ride. Waiting for the train to arrive, we would have a guessing contest about whether it would be a steam locomotive or one of the new diesel engines that were being phased in. Our favourite was the steam locomotive because of the shrill of the whistle as it chugged out of the stations along the way. The only negative was that if you stuck your head out of the window, you were likely to get an eye full of soot which was an unpleasant experience I suffered on a number of occasions, especially in the long dark tunnel between Roma Street and Central stations where in the pitch black much skulduggery was carried out by persons unknown which was fun except if you were the one to get hit over the head.

On the platform at Central stood a couple of coin operated peanut machines containing 'the world's best peanuts from Kingaroy'. Well, that's what the sticker reads that's still stuck firmly across a page in my old 1957 New Testament. The machines required a threepence or sixpence to release the peanuts into a small white paper bag when the knob was turned. The problem was we didn't have any money. Ahhh, but what we did have was a tin button on our shirts which some enterprising young mind quickly worked out would work, if it was flattened. It took quite a few Sundays for the railway staff to deduce who it was that was purchasing the peanuts with buttons and, just when we thought we were on to a good thing, we all received a good dressing down and luckily for us, it was decided to let the matter slide as nobody could prove who the culprits were.

On arrival at church, we sat along the first few pews where we could see in front of us a large carving of the burning bush mentioned in the Old Testament Book of Exodus. It was as if it was looking back at us, reminding us to behave because we were on holy ground. This carving intrigued me, and initially, I thought it was a bit spooky. Suddenly Rev. Peirson would appear and after a call to worship we would sing the opening hymn which was often sung to the Old 100th tune.

"Praise God, from whom all blessings flow, praise Him all creatures here below, praise Him above, ye heavenly host, praise Father, Son and Holy Ghost."

The custom was for us to move to the hall prior to the Pastor's sermon, where we were taught many of the Bible stories and their meaning for us. The lessons were conducted in a manner similar to class instruction at school with exams at the end of the year and there were prizes for the students with the best results. At special times like Christmas we would, as a group, memorise long sections of scripture, each of us learning just a few verses, to be recited out loud to the gathered church from the choir stalls. It could be a nerve-wracking business waiting for your turn and looking at the stony faces of those aptly described dour Presbyterians looking back at you. One of these Christmas church services has remained in my memory. When the boy next to me finished his verses, up I popped and out loud said my piece.

"And the angel said unto them; Fear not: for, behold, I bring you good tidings of great joy, which shall be to all people. For unto you is born this day in the city of David a Saviour, which is Christ the Lord." (Luke 2:10,11)

Feeling relieved at having said my bit I sat, the next boy stood and the message continued. Occasionally, we taught ourselves rhymes to help us remember things taught in class like the names and order of the gospels. One Sunday morning, we were surprised and a little shaken up to hear Rev Peirson let us know that he had heard our gospel rhyme - "Matthew, Mark, Luke and John, hold the horse while I get on. If it bucks, kick it in the guts; Matthew, Mark, Luke and John."

After instructing us about the need to mind our words he sent us off to Sunday School, and I believe I saw a slight smile on his face as we filed out of the church pews.

Due to the long train journey back, lunch, always a cooked meal, was served later than normal and we were usually famished by the time we sat to eat it.

Before and after lunch, we still had our assigned duties to carry out in the dining room and kitchen before we were free to play. One Sunday there was a protest by a boy who had earlier had a lesson on the ten commandments. He said that we should not be doing any work on the Sabbath.

Mr A was outraged by this and made him stand in the centre of the dining room and go without his lunch while he thought about those who had prepared the lunch so that we would not go hungry.

Sundays have remained special for me, for it was on one of those Sundays at Ann Street Presbyterian Church that Mr Dunn, my Sunday school teacher introduced me to Jesus and told me that in Him I could have a friend who would never leave nor forsake me. His words have proved true, and for more than seventy years now Jesus has been my friend. The words of the old hymn have been my lived experience - "On Christ the solid rock I stand, all other ground is sinking sand."

He continues to be the 'bright morning star' who guides me through the storms of life and I am sure will lead me safely home.

CHAPTER 8

HQ BLACKHEATH

They were the days of super heroes in comics and books like *The Secret Seven* and *The Famous Five*. Computers had not arrived on the scene and with no internet, AM Radio ruled the airwaves with programs like *Tarzan, Biggles* and my favourite listened to religiously every afternoon after school, *The Adventures of Hop Harrington*. They were the days of the crystal set made to fit inside a cigar box, matchbox and dinky toy cars.

They were the late 50s and early 60s and boys, especially adventurous younger boys, needed lots of activities to keep them occupied and some might say - out of trouble! Some boyish activities could be a recipe for harmless fun, but others, a recipe for getting into trouble. Put six young rebellious home boys, some ingenuity and some free time into the mix and the outcome often was a full serve of mischief.

Enclosed environments like the Presbyterian-operated Blackheath Boys Home provided all the ingredients needed for the boys to secretly form small clubs or gangs. Many boys felt rejected and lacked self worth having been given an identification number, mine being 36, so being asked to join a club/gang was seen as something special. Membership gave a sense of belonging, particularly when you knew you had been picked over someone else. It was the sort of feeling you get when selected to play in a team sport. You were special in some way and for a boy living in the confines of a boy's home that was a great feeling.

Our gang, six in all, decided we needed somewhere special were we could meet secretly. It would be our HQ (headquarters). From here we could plan amongst other things our war games deciding who would be the Germans and who would be the US Marines to be played out with homemade weapons including, when available, fire crackers like the famous penny bunger and tom thumb, in the out of bounds field of lantana nearby. We settled on an area quite distant from the main house where we hoped we would not be found out. There was a large rectangular hole in the paddock covered in long grass that we decided would make a great HQ if we could get the items to firstly dig it out more and then build a roof over it which would be covered with soil so the grass would grow across it. Nobody except us would know it was there. What a great idea we all agreed!

Where there's a will there's a way! It didn't take long for imagination and effort to find and gather together the materials needed including several large hessian bags nicked from the pantry storehouse, some odd sheets of corrugated iron from an area near where the pigs were kept and some long bits of timber and large tree branches. I have no idea where they came from, but someone produced a few candles and a box of matches for lighting because the only light inside our HQ would be from a small entrance tunnel we had dug down and into the front of the main room.

All six of us were involved in this project and it seems, looking back from the age of seventy-four, that we had it completed in hardly any time at all, but the truth is it probably took us a couple of weeks.

This was now our special meeting place where we quickly discovered after scurrying down the entrance tunnel that the inside was as black as pitch. We definitely needed the light from those candles! Our next discovery was that when all six boys were in this confined area with the candles alight, it wasn't long before it became difficult to breathe and it also became quite hot. We were all too young to have studied physics at school so we didn't realise that our oxygen was quickly being depleted while we were all in there.

And none of us gave a thought to the possibility of the roof caving in and smothering us under its weight.

Then one day when we were crammed into our HQ - it happened!

Not the roof caving in, but a loud gruff and very angry voice demanding that we all come out immediately! "All of you, come out here now!"

We all froze, and for a few moments nobody moved or spoke. We had instantly recognised that voice, it was one that frightened us all because we knew who owned it. It was the voice of the Matron, old Ponka herself, and we all knew she always carried her leather strap with her.

It was our worst nightmare come true! Our HQ had been compromised and the enemy was right outside!

"I won't tell you again!" she blurted out. One by one we crawled out into the open to see her standing astride the entrance complete with her strap over her hip and motioning us with her pointed finger, to stand in a row facing her.

So, there we were, all six of us looking like dirty, sweaty, smelly mud pies that had been baked in an underground oven, waiting to be devoured!

CHAPTER 9

WAR GAMES AND TUNNELS

Young boy,s much like energetic puppies, enjoy playing games, exploring their surrounds and in some cases develop a love for digging as a means of escape. During my middle primary school years, I was one such boy. Together with other like-minded Blackheath boys growing up in the post WWII years, any opportunities to put into practice ideas we came up with were taken advantage of. Many of our ideas had to do with war games and constructing defensive positions which were accessed by making tunnels through the scrub undergrowth and below ground.

The war games involved two sides, one representing the Americans (Yanks), the British (Poms) and Australians (Aussies) and their enemy the Germans (Nazis) and Italians (Ities).

We were completely naive when it came to understanding the ideologies followed by the real participants of WWII or anything about the horrors that wars inflict on people, military and civilian alike. Our understanding came from popular comic books of the time that were filled with unrealistic stories about how the good guys always won the day with very few, if any casualties. Nevertheless, if I'm to be brutally honest, I have to admit that I was initially taken in by the German uniform and flag with their striking colours of black, red and white compared to our drab khaki. I can't remember from where, probably from the dirty washing, but I managed to obtain a black shirt which I kept hidden away for the occasions when I 'went to war' on the German side.

The theatre where we acted out these attacks on each other consisted of a very large block of land that sloped down the hill behind the main house. Much of it was thickly overgrown with lantana about three metres high and which produced a beautiful purple flower. Apart from being strictly out of bounds and capable of causing nasty scratches on the face and legs, the lantana provided the perfect spot for us to form long tunnels through the undergrowth. These tunnels as we called them ended up becoming a maze in which it was easy to lose one's way. To solve this problem we made several sign posts to guide us through the often wet and muddy terrain to our destination, usually a cleared area of a couple of square metres where we held our meetings without the enemy listening in. I remember scrambling through these wet and muddy tunnels and coming upon a y-shaped intersection with a sign which read, 'This way to shit creek'. Well, boys will be boys. I headed off in the other direction!

During a meeting in our lantana hideaway we planned and later dug out a number of trenches down the side of the hill. When the enemy came creeping into range we lit the fuses on our bungers, grenades to us, threw them and then opened fire with the badly constructed wooden rifles we had made. There were loud shouts imitating sub-machine gun fire and outbursts like "Surrender or be killed!"

Things got a bit heated when around cracker night we were able to obtain a few more penny bungers and a few strings of tom thumbs to use as ammo. One of the older boys made a 'Brazooka' a sort of early version of a rocket-propelled grenade launcher. He used a piece of metal water pipe and after stuffing the end with rag put in the gun powder from a few bungers and, then an old spark plug. When the fuse was lit, it went off with quite a loud bang and shot the spark plug into an old forty-four gallon drum standing by the roadside, causing quite a large hole in its side. I sometimes think how very lucky we were that he didn't decide to fire it at the boys coming up the hill toward us and that it didn't backfire and hit one of us standing behind him.

It was only later that I learned that some, I don't know how many, of the fire crackers we used for ammo were purchased with stolen milk money taken from the front steps of local peoples' homes during the night. The culprits were later caught by the police.

On reflection it seemed to me that this is what must have happened as there were way too many fire crackers used in our war games for there not to have been an alternate source of supply. Luckily for me I was not involved, but I was still shaken up to hear that the police were at Blackheath questioning several of the boys about the stolen money. The fear of being sent to live with the Salvation Army or at Westbrook for misbehaving was a constant threat that loomed large in all our minds.

On another occasion I was caught off guard, surrounded and taken prisoner by the Yanks. They tied my arms behind my back and then tied me to an old telegraph pole before interrogating me. They wanted to know where my mates were and which tunnels to follow to find them. But I wasn't going to snitch on my mates, so I didn't tell them anything. They ended up leaving me tied to the pole with tears running down my face while they went into the lantana to search for them. Luckily for me it wasn't too long before a boy who was on my side found and released me.

I later learned from someone at school that the lantana tunnels were being used by some of the older boys as a place to meet with their girlfriends on the weekends, but I wouldn't know about that!

It's amazing to me now, when I think back, that all this was going on just down the hill from the home and yet we were never caught out. Maybe it was because these things mainly happened on the weekends when there was only a skeleton staff on duty.

By far the most dangerous endeavour we undertook was the building of the tunnel right under the main building. Of course we never thought of it as dangerous at the time, only later when we developed some brains! There were about half a dozen of us who after being sworn to secrecy were involved in the digging out of the tunnel. The main difference between this and our earlier constructed HQ mentioned elsewhere, was that this tunnel really was a tunnel dug into the earth below the building. It was very unlikely that Ponka (matron) or anyone else for that matter would find us under the floor. Like the HQ it was constructed by digging a long entrance down on an angle of about thirty degrees till we thought we had gone deep enough. I remember at one stage we had to tunnel around a large post that was in the way. It was hard work removing the soil and spreading it under the building, and it seemed to take ages before we had dug out a space large enough for up to four boys at a time. As with the earlier HQ, we again encountered the problem of not having enough air, which in the end was probably the reason for it not being used as much as we had initially planned. It's one of life's mysteries to me that we weren't caught out, because after crawling out of the tunnel and then out from under the building we were all heavily covered in grey dust - an obvious oversight in our planning!

At Blackheath, there was always some enterprising young mind at work, and I still marvel at the ingenuity of one of our tunnellers who noticed while he was stacking goods into the pantry above the floor near where we had dug the tunnel, that there was a large gap in the floor boards inside the pantry. He decided to place some large cans of tinned fruit over the gap and weigh them down by stacking other cans on top. Later, when we were under the floor, he found the gap and used a sharp implement, I can't remember what, to punch a hole in the tinned pineapple above and then caught the escaping juice in a cup he had taken from the kitchen. How ingenious was that?

I wonder what he went on to do with his life after Blackheath?

No mention of the tinned pineapple with a hole in it ever came to my notice.

Somehow, I survived the Blackheath experience and gained some life skills along the way, though I would not recommend it as a model for raising one's children.

UNEXPECTED

I was up on tip toes and my eyes were anxiously trying to peer sideways over his shoulder. There had been a change in the management at Blackheath and now these words being read to me by the new superintendent were from a letter received from my father. He was asking if Rod and I would like to leave the Blackheath Boys Home and go to live on a sugar cane farm located at a place called Goodwood, south of Bundaberg.

It seems strange to me now, but as a young boy, I was very excited by this letter. I so wanted to see my father's hand writing as the letter was read out to me. This was the first contact received from him in years. I wanted to believe that this letter meant that he hadn't forgotten about us and that he still cared. I was so excited about this letter from my dad that I almost didn't hear the superintendent ask me as the older brother what I thought about the proposed move. However, it didn't take me long to blurt out excitedly that we would be very happy to go. Until at the age of eighteen when I sought written permission from him via grandma Swift to enlist in the RAAF this was the last contact we received from our father.

The next couple of weeks flew by and Rod and I were soon on our way, enjoying the longest train trip we had ever taken. Mr Cane, whom we would soon learn to call 'Dad', met us and travelled with us from Roma Street Railway Station to Goodwood. I recall there was a long stop at the Gympie Railway Station about two hours north of Brisbane. Eventually we arrived at Goodwood, approximately another hour and a half further north and driven to our new home on the sugar farm, passing our new primary school on the way. It all seemed like the adventure of a lifetime to us and I guess to that point in our lives, it was.

On our arrival, Mrs. Cane (Mum to her boys), and we were now her boys too, gave us a warm welcome. She was one of the most warm-hearted people I have met. After showing us to our new digs and introducing us to a couple of the other boys, she asked us to follow her into the kitchen where she explained that she had organised for us to go lobbying along the water holes not far from the house with a couple of the other lads who would show us the ropes.

"Now boys, I want that bucket full when you return and then we will have curried lobbies for dinner," she said with a smile as we disappeared down the back steps armed with small bits of steak tied on strings, a scoop made of fine wire netting, and the bucket. This was our first attempt at lobbying, so Rod and I relied heavily on the other two boys who led the way and showed us how to lure the little creatures out of their mud holes with the bits of steak and scoop them up into the bucket which I am proud to say was around three quarters full by the time we headed back home. True to her word, mum dished up curried lobbies as part of our dinner.

Before dinner and after returning from the creek we met Bruce, Dad's youngest son who was attending the Isis District State High School so he was some years ahead of us. He took a liking to Rodney the moment they met and he nicknamed him Nugget. Bruce spent some time with us both and showed us how to drive the small tractor which we used for various jobs around the farm house. I became very keen about using the *kelpie* as the tractor was known to us, whenever I got the chance, but more of that later.

That evening as we sat at the table for dinner I noticed after grace had been said that unlike Blackheath, we all had the same food, plates and utensils and my eyes were drawn to a rather large plaque on the wall above the sideboard.

The words on the plaque read -

Christ is the Head of this house, the Unseen Guest at every meal. The Silent Listener at every conversation.

It was expected that everyone who lived in the house would read these words often, and live their life accordingly. I remember one evening after dinner when Dad would usually read a story or Bible passage, telling us that although they were both sinful, telling lies was worse than stealing goods from somebody. His reasoning was that it may be possible to retrieve one's goods but once the lie left a person's tongue, the words spoken could never be erased.

FROM BLACKHEATH TO GOODWOOD

Mum and Dad Cane

What a great day I thought to myself that night as I lay quietly in my new bed. Our days at Blackheath were now in the past and I hoped would soon be a distant memory. Clearly that was not to be, for I still remember much from those days nearly seventy years later.

My research revealed that our new address, situated off the Goodwood Road at the end of a long dirt track known as Peirson Road, was known as the Redcliffe Home, Goodwood. During the time I lived there though, I distinctly remember a large sign which had been erected at the entrance of Peirson Road which read - "Heytesbury - Peirson Memorial Training Farm for Boys".

The first four residents were received in 1955, two boys coming from Brisbane and two from Caboolture. These boys apparently were not housed in dormitories, as was the case in many other children's homes throughout Queensland at the time, but had separate bedrooms, each shared between two boys.

I believe we were among the second or third intake of boys, and when we arrived, there was a large room along one end of the house that slept up to six younger boys, another with two older boys and three others on the closed in verandah.

Apparently the land on which the house stands was originally owned by Henry Edward Peirson (born at Heytesbury, Wiltshire, England), and functioned as a sugarcane plantation called Redcliffe Plantation. Following Peirson's death, the property was left to his daughters, who, in 1947 and again in 1953 left it in trust to the Ann Street Presbyterian Church in Brisbane to be run as a training farm for poor boys.

Redcliffe was established in 1955 and licensed as a foster home on 30 September 1955. It was licensed under The Infant Life Protection Act in 1960c., then as a residential institution under the State Children's Act 1911 on 30 April 1964. It was again licensed under the Children's Services Act 1965 on 4 August 1966.

The license granted in 1964 probably explains an issue that I was caught up in with Mr Cane (Dad). Perhaps for some reason he was annoyed with something I had said or done, I don't know, but he let me know very clearly that the Peirson Trust had received no money from our father towards our upkeep and they were having to pay for all our costs as we were not wards of the state. I became quite flustered and said that it was probably because we were really Church of England and not Presbyterians. As one might imagine that went down like a lead balloon!

Frank Cane was the first person appointed to care for the boys at the Redcliffe Home. He had previously served in the army as a chaplain, and had worked in north Queensland with Aboriginal communities.

I recall that each Sunday we were all bundled into the back of the Dodge van and driven down the heavily corrugated gravel

Goodwood Road to church at the small wooden Presbyterian Church. Sometimes if the Pastor was unable to attend dad would take the service. I still recall he liked to speak about Abraham, the man who walked with trust in God. Another memory is that all the children would be locked outside the church whenever the Pastor celebrated the Lord's Supper. We used to climb up on each other's shoulders and try to see through the marbled glass windows what it was they were doing that we weren't allowed to be part of.

I have a couple of photos of the original Redcliffe Home taken in different years and they reveal that quite a bit of restoration and remodelling has taken place over the years since Rod and I were residents there. The oldest photo was taken by Rodney and shows the house as it was when we lived there. The recent photo shows a long building to the rear of the house . (The photos can be viewed on the next page.) This was the old cane cutter's quarters which were removed from the other end of Peirson Road and brought to the present location. I left high school in 1965 and spent a number of weeks working around the property before going to live in Brisbane. One of the jobs I did was to clean up and paint the rooms of the old cane cutters quarters. (1)

Rod's photo taken when we were residents in the early 1960s

The renovated farm house and relocated and renovated cane cutter's quarters

(1) Some factual information above cited at https://findandconnect.gov.au/ref/qld/biogs/QE00526b.htm

CHAPTER 11

FARM LIFE

It had been a wet and freezing cold winter's night. As the dawn approached, the rain had stopped but the wind was still making whistling sounds through the casement windows that lined the verandah on which I and three other older boys slept. I was tucked up under the blankets and not wanting to be disturbed when suddenly there came a voice from beside my bed. It was Bill. "Come on, Swifty, get up or we'll be late to milk the cows!"

Life on the farm was a team effort. We all had our assigned chores to do each day, one of mine just happened to be milking the cows together with a couple of other boys. However, on a wet cold winter's morning it was not my favourite thing, but it had to be done so up I got, and we were soon making our way carrying the milking buckets with the frosty grass cracking under our feet as we walked towards the cow bails. The afternoon before I had rounded up the cows and their calves on Tony the horse and then separated them into two yards for the night, one for the calves and one for the milking cows. So, they were waiting for us with full udders when we arrived to begin milking, and the calves were hungry waiting for what was left when we had finished.

Bill had taught me to milk by hand not long after we arrived at the farm so I became quite good at it over time. I certainly got lots of practice sitting as we did on a piece of tree stump with the bucket between our legs and the cow's tail pinned back on the wall on a six-inch nail. Not all the time was spent squirting milk into the buckets, occasionally someone would get the smart idea to squirt the boy in the neighbouring bail only to find a stream of warm milk coming straight back. Then, it was game on!

By the time we arrived back at the kitchen, there was a hive of industry happening. Some of the boys were making their school lunches, others setting the tables in the dining room for breakfast which always began with one of the boys saying grace and included cereal, eggs, either poached, scrambled, fried or boiled and toast cooked on the combustion stove which had earlier been stoked up and extra fuel added by the rostered boy. I loved it when it was my turn to cook the scrambled eggs in the large iron frying pan on that stove. They were the best scrambled eggs I've ever tasted. All done under the watchful eye of Mum Cane, of course.

We usually brought back two full buckets of milk from the dairy and mum would then separate out any foreigners, such as ticks, by pouring the milk through a cheese cloth into two large white enamel buckets to be placed in the fridge until we returned from school when we would have a glass of milk and bread smeared with jam and cream skimmed off the top of the milk for afternoon tea.

After breakfast, those on kitchen duties cleaned up, washed and dried the dishes while others would be watering the veggie garden and sweeping floors before we all headed to the downstairs bathroom for a wash and the cleaning of teeth etc. before changing into our school uniforms.

When we were ready, dad would have the old Dodge van ready outside the front of the house and we would pile in through the back doors and be seated along two long bench seats, one on each side. Then we were off down the long dirt track over a couple of culverts and onto the main Goodwood Road. If the road had not been graded for some months it became quite corrugated and very dusty which made for a very uncomfortable and bumpy ride to Goodwood State School. On arrival, the primary school boys went into the small two-room school and we high school students waited with some of the other local students for the larger school bus to drive us the half hour or so journey into Childers where we attended the new Isis District State High School. Fortunately this ride was on a bitumen sealed road.

School began very differently in those days I remember. Both at primary and secondary schools, we began on parade where we lined up in order of classes before being addressed by the principal and then stood to attention while the flag was raised and the Australian anthem was played, the boys having first removed their hats which were placed across their left breast. We then filed in an orderly fashion into our class rooms.

At the end of the school day we assembled outside the school gates for the long return journey home to the farm and our awaiting afternoon chores.

Once we were back at the farm, devoured our afternoon tea and changed into some old clothes I was off to find Tony, enticing him up to the yard usually with some left over bread or produce from the veggie garden such as a turnip. Tony was great at doing his job which was to help me find out where in the bush the cows had strayed to during the day and bring them and their calves back to the night yards beside the bails. All I needed to do really was go along for the ride on most days and to hang onto the reins while keeping my head down low so I wouldn't get knocked unconscious or worse by one of the lower tree branches as Tony trotted through the bush.

Having locked the cows and calves in their respective yards, my next job was to power up the pump for the well which would pump water up to the two tanks on stands at the back of the house. Then it was back to my section of the veggie garden to water, weed and pick any items mum required for the kitchen.

My recollection is that apart from free time, most of my daylight hours at home were spent either doing something with the cows or in the veggie patch. I was very proud of my garden, having ploughed the furrows myself with the Kelpie tractor before levelling the red volcanic soil and planting the seedlings. At different times of the year I grew beans, peas, carrots, lettuce, radishes, turnips, cauliflower, cabbages and sometimes a few strawberries and a row or two of potatoes. My favourites were the cauliflowers and the sugar cabbages grown in the cooler months. I always tried to grow them larger than the previous crop. It was a sort of contest I had with myself and one which I believe helped me to win the watch dad Cane promised to give for the best garden for a year.

Saturday mornings until lunch time were spent doing chores that couldn't be done before and after school. One of these was to drive the old Austin ute up along the bush tracks leading off the Goodwood Road in search of firewood for the combustion stove. We took with us a crosscut saw and an axe. We liked to select silky oak trees with a trunk of about ten to twelve inch diameter because they were easy to chop down and cut into lengths suitable to take home on the back of the ute. On arrival back at the farm shed, these were then cut with a large rotary saw into short pieces that we split into two and stacked in rows about one and a half metres high along the rear of the shed until they were required to be taken to the kitchen.

Other chores done on Saturday mornings were the mowing of the lawns around the house, driving the Kelpie tractor around the inside of the large chook pen with the discs fitted to keep the grass and weeds under control, and also there was occasionally the need to spray the cattle for ticks.

Whatever we were doing, the sound of the bell being rung on the back steps meant it was time for us boys to wash up and get ready for dinner.

Later, seated around the dining table Dad would ask one of the boys to say grace and the evening meal would begin following which we usually listened to a Bible story and then it was time to clean up, wash and dry the dishes before completing the necessary ablutions and heading back into the dining room for an hour or two to complete any school homework set for the day.

By the time my head hit the pillow I was usually ready for a good night's sleep. Frequently the next sound I heard came from Bill, "Come on, Swifty, get up or we'll be late to milk the cows!"

The old Dodge van

'Hot Stuff' - The Austin Ute

The Kelpie Tractor

Guy Fawkes with Ian and John

Rod riding Tony near the cow bails

Spraying the cows for ticks

CHAPTER 12

SCHOOL HOLIDAYS

End of year school breakups were always looked forward to and none more so than those I enjoyed while attending Goodwood State Primary School situated a half hour's drive south of Bundaberg. It was a small two-roomed two-teacher school with just enough children around my age to make it an enjoyable experience.

At the end of the school year following the final exams, we would celebrate with games like the three- legged egg and spoon, wheelbarrow and sack races on the oval followed by a special lunch which included a variety of sandwiches and cakes, my favourite being the chocolate crackles and white Christmas slices. This was followed by huge slices of watermelon and other fruits. I recall one year eating so much watermelon under the pine trees in our small school allotment that I felt positively bloated to the point that I thought I might burst if I took another mouthful.

I think the Peirson Trust that ran the sugarcane farm on which we lived preferred, if it was possible for the boys living on the farm to return home or to stay with relatives or friends for the six week holiday break, because each year at this time my brother and I were sent off on the train from Goodwood to Brisbane to stay with our mother, grandfather and uncle Bert at Hendra. The train trip was quite a long one, taking up most of the day with a long stop at the Gympie Railway Station for lunch.

On arrival at Roma Street Railway Station, we were met by Mum, if she was well enough to come to the station, grandad who we also knew as Pop and Uncle Bert. Mum's teary face would be positively beaming when she saw us coming off the train toward her. She would wrap her arms around us, give us the biggest kiss and hug ever while telling us how much she loved and missed us.

Usually we would travel home in Pop's old grey Humber super snipe car, though I do recall one year being driven home in a borrowed ute with a tied down canvas cover. The tail gate was lowered and we were told to climb in under the cover and the tail gate was locked back in place - we couldn't see a thing! Before he drove off, Pop tapped the side of the ute and said "Ok, boys, we're off home, now I want you to remember until we get home, not a sound from either of you!"

As a young lad living away from home, I loved these holidays because I felt a sense of belonging to a family. Around Christmas time the wider family would usually come together even if only for a few days. It was great; there would be uncles and aunts and cousins from Lismore, Charleville and Cairns and sometimes the mob from Scarborough. The adults would fill the kitchen and dining rooms telling yarns, drinking beer and eating oysters and salami sausage before sitting around the dining room table which was covered with a large army war surplus blanket and the *poker* game would begin. Match sticks or threepences and sixpences were used to bet with. Meanwhile, we kids ran amok playing our own games.

When we weren't chasing each other around the house and yard with the occasional bark from an adult or two to calm down, we enjoyed passing the time playing board games, the most popular being *Test Match, Monopoly, Snakes and Ladders, Ludo, Chinese Checkers* and *Draughts*. We played *Test Match* so often that we wore out the board! I loved bowling Uncle Bert out with a full toss, almost as much, I think now, as he loved playing with us kids. Sometimes there would be a small wager, and if we bowled his team out first, we were up for a large two bob bottle of Coke and a Cherry Ripe.

In those days, before Grandma Becker succumbed to asthma, Christmas dinners were something to behold. Grandma and Mum would be busy in the kitchen from early in the morning baking the roast chickens and vegetables and mixing up the plum pudding into which were inserted threepences for us to find later hopefully without breaking a tooth. If we were lucky, we would be invited to lick the remaining pudding mixture from the mixing bowl and spoon.

A few days before Christmas Day, Grandad would have arrived home in the Humber after going for a drive up the highway, with a pine tree hanging out the back window. The tree was planted into a bucket wrapped with red crepe paper before being decorated with tinsel and coloured balls and crowned with a large glittering star. On Christmas morning a few wrapped presents, usually books, board games and sweets, would be found under the tree for the children spending Christmas at Grandad's home.

I loved sitting at the large dining room table for Christmas lunch with my extended family and sharing in the chicken roast and plum pudding smothered with custard and cream. It was my favourite meal of the year even though it was usually eaten on a very hot and humid day. I recall how quiet the afternoons were following Christmas lunch. All the adults retired for an afternoon nap and we children were left to entertain ourselves as long as we were quiet and didn't wake Pop.

A few days later, when the relatives had all gone home things would settle down somewhat and Rod and I would spend hours reading popular comics of the day, such as *The Phantom, The Flash, Superman, Batman* and other favourites. We purchased many of these with money we obtained by returning empty soft drink bottles to the local milk bar, and some came from pocket money given to us by Uncle Bert, usually on Saturdays to keep us out of Grandad's hair until he arrived home from work in the afternoon. In those days the shops stayed open till midday on Saturdays, and Bert worked as manager of the carpet department at the Waltons store across the road from the Prince of Wales Hotel. Pop would often do a bit of grocery shopping before meeting him there for a couple of beers before driving home in the car. When they did arrive home somewhat tipsy from the - 'couple of beers,' Bert would often crash on one of the club lounge chairs before offering us boys two bob each to take his shoes and socks off his hot and smelly feet! We didn't mind at all, two bob was a lot of money to us so we were eager to comply with his request.

On other occasions we would set up a game of bobs on a table out on the front verandah, and then challenge Uncle Bert to a game or three with the winner getting a shilling or two as prize money. I'm still not sure if he couldn't shoot straight with the cue because he had sunk a few too many at the Prince of Wales or he just wanted us to win, but it was great fun and we lapped up the attention.

Most nights after dinner, dishes and a bath we watched the new addition to the house, - Black and White TV!

Before Bert got the idea of renting the TV, Rod and I would trot up to the Lonergan's home a few doors up the street for a couple of hours to watch their television, and I still remember watching my first TV show, *Superman* which ran for fifteen minutes. This was followed by my favourite, *The Rifleman* starring Chuck Connors. Wow, what Chuck could do with that repeating Winchester rifle. I thought he was much more interesting than *The Lone Ranger* with his silver bullets fired from a revolver.

Back at Grandad's house we watched the rented AWA twenty four inch TV which required a couple of two shillings and later twenty cent coins to be inserted into a slot in a metal box at the back of the TV before we could view a show. I recall how frustrating it was for all of us when the last twenty cent piece dropped down and the screen went blank in the middle of a good show. However, not to be outdone my youngest brother Greg secretly found a solution to this problem. He worked out how to stick a kitchen knife up into the box from the bottom to release a couple of twenty cent pieces which he then recycled through the slot at the top and presto, we once again had a working TV! What we didn't know at the time was that the sneaky little devil pocketed more coins than he recycled! This only worked until the rental company representative arrived to find the box almost empty which somehow didn't tally up with the number of hours supposedly viewed.

We enjoyed many hours seated around this black and white TV watching shows like *Combat, Bonanza, Rawhide, Gilligan's Island* and *McHale's Navy*. Rod really loved Captain Binghamton who always failed to catch the others of the patrol boat crew out for being involved in some mischief or other. *The Three Stooges* also got a lot of laughs. In my opinion though none of them came close to The Rifleman.

These Christmas school holidays were 'happy days' (pun intended), and I can hardly believe now that we were watching these old TV favourites while seated around a twenty-four inch (before metric) television with an indoor antenna that quite often failed to produce a picture devoid of snow. It was made all the more enjoyable, however, when Uncle Bert arrived home with a two-bob Coke and his pockets, full of Cherry Ripes, Violet Crumbles, Mars bars etc. and blurting out in a loud and jolly tone - " Boys, let's have a party tonight while we watch TV!"

We knew he'd been to the Prince of Wales!

But, as the old saying goes, "all good things come to an end" and too soon it seemed the school holidays had flown by and we were once again on the train heading north to Goodwood for another year at school and life on the farm.

Mum, Uncle Bert holding Greg, Rod front left, John on right.

Grandad (Pop) holding Greg on a visit to Charleville

CHAPTER 13

PRIMARY SCHOOL DAYS

All around me there were children crying and a couple throwing tantrums, while others including myself and Kay, my friend and next door neighbour were watching on. Memorably, this was my first day at primary school. I had been looking forward to it for some time having missed out on the opportunity to attend kindergarten but, I never thought it would begin like this. Just inside the classroom entrance there were a couple of mothers trying to disengage themselves from their children who were clinging on to their skirts while a member of the school staff was attempting to assure them that all would be just fine if they left the children and went home. Meanwhile Mrs. Rayner, my year one teacher, was trying to entertain the rest of us by drawing elephants with big ears and long trunks on the blackboard.

Nundah State School still stands as it did then. A red brick fortress is how I remember it. The large WWI cannon placed across from the front entrance did help to give that impression to a young five year old boy. Still today, I have fond memories of the large playing fields and the wattle trees that were truly spectacular in bloom along the school fence line. I attended this school with Mrs. Rayner as my teacher for grades one and two before my mother became ill and the family separated which resulted in a change of schools, the first of many.

There are only now a few memories I have of my time at Nundah State School. The clearest of these is of going to school on the school bus. All the children used to like teasing the bus driver whose name was George by saying out loud in the bus the nursery rhyme 'Georgy porgy pudding and pie, kissed the girls and made them cry. When the boys came out to play Georgy porgy ran away'.

Another memory is having to line up in single file in front of an elderly man (he probably wasn't that old) seated on a chair to be tested for our vocal ability. This man decided whether or not we would sing in the school choir. I was not selected!

This school also had quite a large fife band that played music each morning as we marched from the parade ground into our classrooms. I was not in this either.

After leaving Nundah State School I soon found myself living on the other side of Brisbane where my younger brother and I were residents at Blackheath Boys Home from where I attended Corinda State School. This was a very different school structurally being a highset timber building with verandahs running along the front of the classrooms. Underneath was a bitumen floor providing a space for the children to eat lunch and stay out of the hot sun and rain. This place was also where each child received their half pint bottle of milk each day supplied by the Queensland Government to all primary school children. Across the road was a small shop where children with a shilling or two could buy lunch and a drink and maybe one of the new flavoured straws to drink their school milk with. I never had any reason to visit that shop, though I would have liked to try one or two of their cream buns!

My classroom windows still had the blackout paint and tape on some of them. This had been done during the second world war, to prevent light from being seen by enemy aircraft and was a vivid memory of earlier troubled times.

Corinda State Primary School also has a place in my memories because it was there that I first experienced the sting of the principal's cane across my hand. I had been sitting quietly in the year four class learning to sing the song *Old Father Thames* being taught to us by Mrs Thompson when somebody behind me made a rude noise. The teacher, who was crabby at the best of times looked up and asked who had done it. Nobody owned up so she picked me and told me to leave the room and stand outside the door. As luck would have it the principal, a tall slender man with jet black hair which he wore in the fifties fashionable crew cut style, happened to be walking along the verandah and on seeing me standing outside told me to get myself to his office pronto. He arrived shortly after and said I must have done something very wrong to have been sent out of the class. He ordered me to hold my hand out and the next thing I knew he had picked up his cane and brought it down across my hand. Ouch! It really hurt! He told me to get back to class and behave myself in future or I would be back for more. I remember this incident because what hurt more than my stinging fingers was the fact that it had all been unjust as I hadn't done anything wrong. I really was an innocent victim. It was one of my early experiences that taught me life is not fair.

All, however, was not gloom and doom as on the day when I had been carrying out my duties as an ink monitor, I found a nice shiny sixpence on the ground. I have no idea now what I spent it on but it was probably peanuts at Central Railway Station one Sunday on the way to church. Other memories regarding my time at Corinda are mentioned elsewhere so I will not retell them here.

I once worked out that in total I experienced a minimum of eight moves during my primary school years, so now my memory is a little hazy as to when I was where. There is, however, a clear recollection of initially spending about a year at Corinda before going to Ascot Primary School where I learned to swim in the school pool and for a short while attending Redcliffe Primary School where I once missed catching the school bus home which created quite a stir when I still hadn't arrived home about two hours later. The truth is that I got lost on the way to Auntie Myrtle's home where I was staying with my mother at the time and on arriving home I heard the adults talking about notifying the police before setting out to look for me. Frightened by what I had heard, I hid in the upstairs storeroom amongst the bags of onions and potatoes for about an hour or so before coming out to announce I was home. After the relief on the adults faces subsided Uncle Kel told me that the police were looking for me so I had better catch the bus and be home on time in the future. For about the next six months I kept an eye out for any police wherever I went.

After living at Scarborough and attending Redcliffe Primary School, I went for a brief time to live with my dad who had built a new family home for us and which shared a back fence with my new school at Geebung. I think this must have been a last attempt by my dad to heal the family. I remember him asking me what I would like on my sandwiches for school lunch. Peanut paste ended up being the choice and then every day until the bottle was empty I took peanut paste sandwiches to school. This was followed by cheese spread and yes, I had cheese spread sandwiches every day until there was none left in the jar. Going to school each day was easy. Dad left for work quite early in the mornings leaving me alone in the house. When it came time to go, all I had to do was lock the back door of the house and climb over the cyclone wire fence along the back boundary of our property then walk across the playing fields to my classroom. After school, Dad would usually come by the house and together we would go on his radio repair rounds sometimes bringing a radio or two home with us in the back of his Morris van. Sadly a couple of months later everything fell apart, and once more my younger brother Rod and I soon found ourselves living back at the Blackheath Boys Home which meant returning to Corinda State Primary School for part of years five and six.

In the second half of year six, we again moved from Blackheath to live at Goodwood where Rod and I attended a small two-room country primary school. The classes were divided into two groups with years one to four in one room and the rest, years five to eight in the other. I remember the school having a small pine forest and we were taught forestry as a subject, something I enjoyed very much. Grade eight was made all the more interesting because one day every week we were driven by bus into Childers about half an hour's drive to learn woodwork at the newly built Isis District State High School. The manual arts teacher I remember was a most gentle and patient man, taking time to explain how things were to be done and showing the boys by example how to use the various woodwork tools. I liked him a lot.

Life became much more settled once we arrived at Goodwood and it was there at the end of year eight that I sat for the scholarship exam that all Queensland students had to pass in order to attend high school. The following year, having passed the scholarship exam, I became a student at the new Isis District State High School — once more a new boy in a new school, but this time I was only one of many new year nine students.

CHAPTER 14

THE HIGH SCHOOL YEARS
(1963 - 1965)

L ife, I have found, is made up of many new beginnings and starting high school was one. After eight years of attending primary school dressed in a pair of boxer shorts and T-shirt, putting on the new high school uniform complete with felt hat, school tie, badge, and black lace-up shoes made one feel rather special. Also, the journey to the Isis District State High School at Childers in the school bus that picked us up from outside the Goodwood Primary School added another thirty minutes travelling time which made going to and from school somewhat of a new adventure for the first few weeks.

The first day especially was all rather exciting. On arrival all the new students were seated in a large room and grouped into various classes according to the course chosen. We were asked to indicate by a show of hands which course we would be studying. The choice for me was between the industrial course and the academic course. Initially, I raised my hand for my name to be included with the academic students as I thought that subjects like French, History and Geography sounded very interesting indeed. But then I noticed that my only friend in the room raised his hand to study in the industrial course. In fact, almost all the boys in the room had opted for the industrial course because it included the subjects of wood work, metal work and technical drawing all of which would be helpful in obtaining an apprenticeship after successfully completing the Junior exam the following year. Suddenly my hands were in the air waving madly to grab the teacher's attention so I could explain that I had made a mistake and should have been listed with the boys in the industrial class. The real reason of course was I simply wanted to be in my mate's class.

I sometimes wonder about the different path my life might have taken had I stayed with my first choice and studied history, something I have enjoyed reading for much of my adult life.

Initiations are often part of being welcomed into group settings and students beginning high school are often prime targets. It was only a couple of days into the school year when suddenly towards the end of the lunch period, a number of older boys surrounded our group on the freshly mowed football oval. It was a hot summer's day and we were all rather sweaty from playing on the oval when I was grabbed and held down while grass was stuffed down my shirt, my shoes were taken off, tied to another boy's shoes and thrown across the oval. This happened to about half a dozen of us 3B boys with only about five minutes for us to be back in class.

Fortunately for us, arriving back in the class room about ten minutes late and still itching from the grass down our backs, the teacher took a dim view of what had taken place so there were no punishments handed out to us on that occasion.

When I get hair down the back of my collar at the barber shop and it itches, I often think of the grass I had stuffed down my shirt on that hot summer's day and how I couldn't wait to get home to have a wash.

Memories of my high school years are mostly to do with the sporting activities I participated in. Rugby and cricket took up a lot of my time though I was never much good at cricket when compared to some of the other boys who constantly bowled me out in the house matches. On two occasions I remember leaving the field because of injuries, one being the result of a full toss bowled by a fast bowler by the name of Mick, that I tried to block only to have the cricket ball hit the end of the bat and run straight up into my nose. The other was a fast paced bowl straight into my shin bone - now that also really hurt!

Rugby, at which I was somewhat gifted was my preference over cricket. I usually played as the full back changing with lock and sometimes in a forward position in the Pindar House matches. On more than one occasion, I remember being the cause of penalties given against our team because I had the bad habit of grabbing the ball out of the scrum and passing it to my mate Greg who played very well as half back and would often score a try if we were close to the goal line. Overall, I believe I was a reasonably good rugby player, often scoring a try in the matches I played in and together with a few others received a mention in the 1964 school magazine in relation to the house and inter school rugby matches. Though we were often soundly beaten on the scoreboard, the school bus trips away to Gladstone, Mackay and Hervey Bay were great times. Sometimes the girl's netball teams travelled on the bus with us and all I can say about that is that what went on in the back of the bus stays in the bus!

On the athletics field I was more gifted in the running events especially over the shorter distances such as the one hundred and two hundred yard races, though I seem to remember that we all ran in the cross country event at the completion of the day in the house sports competitions. Other events I remember entering were the shot put and long jump. I was too short for the high jump!

As part of the industrial class, I enjoyed making things in the woodwork and metalwork classes especially if a lathe was used. In my wardrobe I still have a wooden coat hanger for which the teacher gave a mark of 85% and a jewellery box with dovetailed corners made from silky oak that I gave to mum that Christmas. Perhaps the most difficult project we completed was a three foot six inches tall wooden step ladder that I later sold to a man for the princely sum of ten dollars. Also, using the wood lathe I turned out a rather solid rolling pin which was then used in our kitchen.

Metalwork also involved using the lathe to turn various objects but the thing I remember most from metalwork was making a large tin coffee mug. I have no idea where it is now!

Technical drawing was a subject that I grew to like very much especially when we began to learn drawing in perspective. The hardest part of tech drawing was trying to keep my sweaty arms and hands from smudging the pristine white drawing paper when we began the class after lunch.

English was something I enjoyed immensely. Writing essays was always challenging and acting in various roles in plays was always great fun. I remember playing Julius Caesar wearing a white toga splattered with blood and several cardboard daggers stuck to my back. My part was to look at Brutus with a look of agonising dismay and yell "Et tu Brute`?" (even you Brutus?) and then to fall down dead . To do this I was required to fall across a low table so that the audience could still see me. Having fallen I noticed my arm was swinging like a pendulum. Lest the audience should think I wasn't really dead, I slowly brought it to a stop which caused some laughter from those watching in the first few rows.

Physics was another of my favourite subjects during year 10. Building electronic circuits really struck a chord with me, especially when we used valves such as when building a power supply. I couldn't wait to learn more about the field of electronics since I was beginning to think seriously about becoming an apprentice radio technician so that I could build and repair radio equipment just like my dad. In fact, it was around this time that I agreed to forgo sixteen weeks of pocket money in order to purchase my very first transistor radio. The sacrifice was worth it and that little HMV Transistor Radio became my most prized possession for several years though I almost lost it for good a few weeks after purchasing it.

I took it to school with me and a group of us were sitting under a tree during the lunch break listening to the Seekers sing their song "I'll never find another you" when suddenly the principal appeared as if from nowhere and demanded to know who owned the radio.

I owned up and he told me to give it to him and that I could see him after school in his office.

I was devastated! What was so wrong about taking my transistor radio to school? All afternoon in class I thought about nothing else but whether or not he was he going to give me back my radio? Straight after my last class I made my way to the principal's office expecting to be told off and probably receive the cane but I thought it would all be worth it if I got the radio back.

When I arrived at the office, I noticed as I stood in the open doorway that there was nobody in the office and there sitting on the end of the desk was my radio. I looked around me, nobody was in sight so, after a slight hesitation, I quickly went in grabbed the radio and took off down the verandah and out of the school grounds and radio in hand, safely made it to the school bus. I never took the little transistor radio to school again and the principal must have forgotten about it as he never mentioned anything about the radio to me.

Though I sometimes enjoyed algebra and geometry, maths was eventually to become my downfall at high school. Nothing seemed to go well for me in maths class. On one occasion when I had failed to get the correct answer the teacher yelled at me in front of the whole class, "Typical of the place you come from!" I was deeply hurt but said nothing. One of the girls in the class went home and that night told her father, who just happened to be a solicitor, what the teacher had said. He in turn phoned Mr Cane who then gave me a dressing down for not telling him about the incident as the teacher's comments had he said, brought disrepute on the Peirson Farm and all who lived there. The next day with me in tow he visited the school principal and explained what had taken place and demanded a public apology by the teacher in front of the school assembly. All I could think was that the maths teacher was going to kill me when I went back to class.

There never was a public apology given, though I heard that the teacher concerned did apologise to Mr Cane in the principal's office, but I don't know if that's true or not.

As one might imagine, things did not improve for me in maths that year and in the following year calculus proved a great challenge and rather than obtaining help from the teacher, I again received his condemnation. I later heard that he had written the calculus curriculum so maybe he took it personally that I found it so difficult to follow. His assessment of my work in the mid year report was that in his opinion the level of work was beyond my ability.

In the Junior exam the previous year, I had achieved five Bs and three Cs, more than enough for entry into a trade apprenticeship so after a short discussion with Dad, I began to think that school was not for me and in the second half of the sub-senior year (1965), I left school and spent some weeks working around the farm before getting a ride to Brisbane with Bruce who had been home on leave from the army before being posted to Vietnam.

In Brisbane, Bruce dropped me on the footpath outside my grandfather's home and sped off down the road in his Austin Healey sports car never to be seen by me again.

So there I was sixteen years old standing on the footpath with no money, holding a small school port containing a change of clothes and my precious transistor radio.

I had no idea what lay ahead. I certainly had no idea that my Grandfather who was enjoying his afternoon nap was not expecting me, but this and all of the events that followed, well that's another story!

4B 1964. John front left next to Greg, also from the farm. John's mate Greg back row, second from right.

ADDITIONAL REFLECTIONS

CHAPTER 15

HEALTH MATTERS

She caught me by the arm, only just, but she managed to get a firm grip just above the elbow as I was about to flee down the front steps to freedom.

As a young child I was quite often in poor health suffering mainly from asthma which landed me in the Children's Hospital on at least one occasion and maybe more though the memories are now a bit blurred. The doctor was concerned about how thin and frail I looked, and to help me, he had advised my mother to try and build me up by feeding me a thick malt syrup known as molasses. It came in a large brown coloured glass jar.

I recall how very large for my small mouth the spoon was that mum used to feed this into me. My guess is that with me throwing a tantrum and trying to escape her hold on me, she wanted to make sure she would get as much syrup as possible into me in one go.

And so, even though I put up quite a fight, there on the front steps of our home in Shaw Road for all the world to see, in went the spoon resulting in syrup dripping down my chin.

Memories of this torturous process go back to around the age of three (1952).

Some bouts of asthma were quite debilitating and a common occurrence I experienced was being held out of the bedroom window so that I could breathe the fresher outside air which it was hoped would help ease my wheezing. Wheezing was always a problem that seemed to make my condition worse. To help with this the doctor had instructed mum to give me liberal amounts of lemonade to drink. If there was any benefit to suffering from asthma, drinking lemonade was surely it!

Being a young child my parents would, if I was having trouble breathing, put me in their bed so that they could, in a manner of speaking, keep an eye on me. The problem was I would constantly crawl up to the top of the bed and lie across the pillows where it was cooler, but which left very little room for two adults to sleep comfortably. This resulted in a poor night's sleep for all and rather tired and grumpy parents the next morning!

There was one incident that took place in my parents bedroom that has always perplexed me. I have never thought of myself as superstitious or someone who is overly mystical. On the contrary, I have always tended toward a rational explanation for the unexplained. This incident is however indelibly printed on my brain from all those years ago and other than being an experience of hallucination, it defies a rational explanation.

It happened one night when I was ill and had been placed in my parents bed with a couple of pillows to prop me up. Suddenly as I looked up toward the window, there she was, a kindly looking old woman with a shawl around her shoulders was looking at me through the bedroom window. But without a ladder that was impossible, I knew that nobody was that tall. I know it's spooky, well it was for me with my eyes fixed on the image before me. She said nothing, just smiled and then she disappeared and I have never seen her again. Was it hallucination? As far as I remember I was not suffering from a fever. Who was she?

I have never been able to find a rational explanation.

What it must be like to go to hospital was not something I often dwelt on, but it had crossed my mind once or twice. I was to find out the real thing was nothing like my thoughts about it.

I was about the age of eight or nine, by which time I was living as a resident of the Blackheath Boys Home with my younger brother Rodney. Our mum had suffered a nervous breakdown and was no longer able to care for us, while our father had gone to live with another woman, and after we had been placed at Blackheath had nothing further to do with us.

I had been feeling unwell for a couple of days and the matron decided that I should be taken to visit the local doctor. On arrival at the surgery with a Blackheath staff member, I was made to wait for quite some time before eventually being called in to the doctor's room. He examined me for a short time before calling in his assistant and instructing her to phone an ambulance saying, "this lad is quite sick, I believe he has measles and has developed pneumonia judging by the sound of his lungs, his temperature is high and his lips are purple. He needs hospitalisation." I remember my breathing was quite laboured by this time, maybe because I was quite anxious about what was happening.

Shortly later the ambulance arrived, I was placed in the back and off we went with me having no clue really as to where they were taking me.

That I was concerned about what was happening would be an understatement but somehow I managed to keep it together until we arrived at our destination - The Princess Alexander Hospital.

Because I had overheard the doctor talking to his assistant I remember worrying about what pneumonia was. I knew it must be serious because he had sent me to a hospital. "Was I going to get better?" was the question that kept running through my mind.

It wasn't long before two wardsmen had bundled me out of the ambulance and onto a trolley, then we were off down the hospital corridor to an awaiting bed, my home for the next week or thereabouts.

After changing into hospital pyjamas, a nurse tucked me into bed after pulling the curtains around it to give me some privacy. Then after mentioning that the doctor would visit me shortly, she was gone.

I must have slept soundly for my next memory is waking the next morning. The curtains were no longer around the bed which gave me a full view of the ward and its patients. It didn't take long to realise that I was by far the youngest patient there, all the rest being adults. I don't know why, but initially I found it frightening to be in this large ward with all these strange men.

Breakfast, which was much better than at Blackheath, arrived very early and not long after the doctor came by with a small group of people tagging along.

Hospitals, I soon learned, are very busy places with people coming and going all day long except when the nurse announced it was rest time. Then, in the early evening during visiting hours the ward became a buzz with visitors.

The patient in the bed to my left was visited every day by his wife who always brought him reading material and various food stuffs. On about the third evening, I overheard him quietly telling her that I had not had any visitors since I had arrived in the ward. The next day she came bearing gifts for me as well as her husband. I thought they were a kind couple and very much enjoyed the biscuits, fruit and sweets she gave me, but back then I was a very shy boy and found it difficult to say much more than thank you.

The only other visitor I had during my stay was from a priest - a hospital chaplain, I now think. Towards the end of the visiting time I had dropped off to sleep only to be suddenly woken up by a voice coming from beside my bed. I remember well opening my eyes to see an old man bent over and looking down at me. He was dressed in black with a white collar around his neck. I must admit, I got the shock of my life seeing him there. He smiled at me, asked a few questions, said a few things that I quickly forgot and then he was gone. It was all rather odd.

During the next couple of days my health greatly improved and then late one afternoon another couple of wardsmen appeared with a trolley to move me to another ward.

At first I thought that I might be going back to Blackheath, but when we were in the lift it went up, not down. They delivered me to a ward where it seemed to me that everyone I could see was in traction. There were arms and legs in the air everywhere. Now I was scared! Two nurses were making up my bed as we arrived and I noticed them slip a large flat board under the mattress. As they tucked me in I heard one of them say "poor little fellow".

I didn't want to be strung up like the others I could see. What, I wondered was going to happen to me? Why was I brought here? I was sure I was getting better but now it seemed that maybe they were going to operate on me.

I was still anxiously lying there about an hour later when two irate men appeared in the ward. One was cursing the stupid person who had mistakenly taken a young patient to the wrong ward.

Whew! What a relief it was to discover that I should have been given a bed in the transit ward on the verandah. Patients in this ward were there only briefly before being discharged.

How glad I was to arrive in the transit ward, words cannot describe.

Next morning I was back in an ambulance on my way to Oxley, and the following day it was back to school - all cured!

As I grew into my teenage years it seemed as though my asthma and visits to hospitals was going to be a thing of the past. Maybe it had something to do with all the sport and other activities young people take on. I did spend a lot of time playing football, working around the farm, riding the horse, rounding up the milking cows after school, swimming in the river and lagoon and taking long walks through the bush on weekends and later still after leaving school, I spent many weekends surfing on the Gold Coast.

There were a few times, however, when I was laid up for a few days not feeling one hundred percent fit. One occasion was after the school sports carnival. Not thinking about the consequences, I entered into the one hundred, four hundred and eight hundred yards races and then later ran in the cross country event after which my legs became very sore indeed. The next morning I could barely stand up let alone walk. So, after being told how stupid I had been by running in so many events I was kept home from school to rest.

If memory serves me correctly, my next health calamity happened around the age of thirteen. Saturday had started out as a very pleasant sunny day. We had been driven down to Woodgate beach for a day out swimming and a barbecue lunch. Back then Woodgate had a couple of swimming enclosures as well as a large weatherboard changing shed. It was divided into two sections and was in desperate need of repair being held up by several large wooden beams along the back wall. To the rear of this shed was a BBQ area. Everyone was having a great time in the water until someone spotted a couple of sharks swimming around the outside of the old wooden enclosure. There were a couple of large gaps below the waterline so the enclosure wasn't all that safe. A couple of us boys decided to collect some large stones, climb out on the edge of the enclosure wall and use the sharks for target practice. Maybe that would scare them away and we could safely resume swimming. It was a ridiculous plan and the sharks didn't take any notice.

The barbecue itself was rather basic, a couple of cemented rock walls supporting a couple of large metal plates, one for the fire and a top plate to cook on. Previous users had left some firewood and we had brought some kindling to get the fire going.

Suddenly, just as the fire was taking hold, there was a creaking sound coming from the change shed and then the whole back wall fell out to the sound of shrieks from the half dressed and naked women inside.

I remember we teenagers thought it was very funny until one of the oldies pulled us back into line saying "What's so funny? Someone could have been seriously hurt!"

The women soon regained their composure and everyone calmed down as the smell of the barbecue began to claim our attention.

It was about this time when I remember beginning to feel very sore under my left arm. I had received a vaccination for smallpox a couple of days earlier and now I was beginning to suffer the after effects. It's not something I would wish on anyone, in fact it became one of the most painful things I had experienced to date. My temperature skyrocketed and my left armpit became completely swollen for the next few days. Well that was the end of my day at the beach!

During the next week while recovering in bed I somehow managed to read through two popular books of the day, *The Cruel Sea* and *Zulu*.

Eventually the pain eased, the swelling went down and after a couple more days of rest all was back to normal, and that meant back to school!

CHAPTER 16

TWO OR THREE A PENNY?

It was before the mighty dollar and it was for most families before double incomes. The norm for most families was that dad worked and mum stayed at home with the kids. It was a time when it was still worth stooping to pick up a sixpence or even as in my case, the occasional threepence spotted lying on the ground. I recall the primary school principal instructing me to "Lift up your head as you walk along young man, there is no threepence to be found on the ground today!" Life was certainly different back then in the early 1950s.

I've heard it said many times by elderly folks from back then, that they can't remember what happened yesterday or last week, but they have a clear recollection of what happened all those decades ago when they were young.

I also recall some of these earlier times when as a very young boy I lived in our family home at Shaw Rd, Wavell Heights. The home was a newly built war service home, one of many in the area. The property was quite large, facing onto two streets and has long since been subdivided. My father had not long been demobbed from the army and, I am told, threatened to turn it into a compound by running barbed wire around the top of the fence to keep me from leaving the property.

Back then Wavell Heights was an outer suburb with much of the land on the northern side of Edinburgh Castle Rd, just up from us covered in long grass, groundsel and lantana. It was a favourite place for the young boys of the neighbourhood to play Cowboys and Indians. Davey Crockett was every boy's hero and we boys wore coonskin caps like his, although ours were made from wallaby skins. *The Battle of the Alamo* was my favourite movie. It told the story of how our heroes Davey Crockett, Jim Bowie and a few other Texans held up the advancing Spanish Army under the command of Santa Anna until eventually the Alamo was overrun.

There were not many shops near our home, so a big celebration was called when a small shopping centre complete with an Ampol Service Station was opened in Shaw Rd opposite the Villeroy St intersection. Opening Day was celebrated with streamers and balloons as well as ice creams, lollies and soft drinks for the children and speeches were given but I was too taken with my fairy floss to be interested in listening to what grownups had to say about the shops etc.

My most popular shop was the general store operated by Mr and Mrs Addlington. I recall my father sending me to purchase a tube of tooth paste. When I arrived Mrs Addlington asked me which one I wanted and I couldn't remember. I had a choice of Ipana, Colgate or a new one, McLeans. I thought dad would like the peppermint taste described to me, so that was the one I chose. WRONG! My father wanted nothing but Colgate and I was not a popular boy.

Mrs Add, as she was affectionately known by all the children in the area was one of the most patient people I've met. Taking a small white paper bag from a hook on the wall, and standing behind her famous lolly counter, she would serve us, but her rule was strictly - "only one at a time!"

Some thirty years later, I was back in the area and couldn't resist a visit to the old shop which I was surprised to see was still there. More surprising, when I stepped inside, was that an elderly Mrs Add was still behind the counter! I noticed her looking at me for a few moments before bursting out with "I know you, you're little Johnny Swift, aren't you"? I couldn't believe it, after all those years.

"You used to come in here, with your threepence or sixpence and stand in front of the glass and point out to me which lollies you wanted to buy. You used to say, I'll have a penny's worth of those clinkers but then you'd notice that the lollies in the next box, maybe freckles, milk bottles or mint leaves etc. were three a penny not two, and you'd change your mind. If you had sixpence to spend, I'd be there for ages while you worked out how to get the absolute best value for your money!"

I thought about the times I had done this and particularly the times when during the transaction, I had wanted to make another last minute change to purchase my favourite - those delicious musk sticks, but couldn't afford them and the lollies Mrs Add had already placed in the paper bag for me. We stood there smiling at each other, and both of us burst into a slight chuckle.

They were some of the happiest days! They were followed by not so happy times, but by God's grace and good providence both Rod and I have come through these difficult years and gone on to live full meaningful lives.

CHAPTER 17

FINAL WORDS

"How will I know when the book is finished?" "Only you will know that, but you will know when it's time to stop," my writing group coordinator said in reply.

The manuscript for this book has sat on the corner of my desk for several months now with me feeling that something more needs to be said. But what?

Although the purpose in writing this book has been to describe my early years while growing up in institutional care, I have come to realise that having accomplished this, it would be remiss of me to leave the reader wondering, by not saying something about how life unfolded for the young lad left standing on the footpath outside his grandfather's home after leaving school and life on the Goodwood farm.

So, the following is a brief sketch of how life unfolded.

Within a few days I found employment as an apprentice electrician at a local electrical repair shop within walking distance of grandad's home. Then several months later after not enjoying the work, I managed to gain employment as a junior clerk for the Brisbane City Council in the Health Department with the prospect of becoming a cadet health inspector in the near future. What I didn't know was that another young man whose father was one of the BCC health inspectors was also interested in the cadetship. He was successful in obtaining the position which left me as the junior clerk.

Some time later, with conscription on the horizon due to the conflict in Vietnam, I took the opportunity to enlist in the RAAF as a radio technician adult trainee. My RAAF service was from 1967 to 1973 during which time I served at various bases around Australia working on fire truck radios, overseas broadcast transmitters, radio receivers of various kinds and for a couple of years as a CADF (commutated aerial direction finding equipment) installation and maintenance technician.

Enlisting in the RAAF was probably one of the best decisions I could have made at that time. It helped an innocent and rather naive young man to mature, to become independent and to learn to make responsible decisions. Most importantly to me at the time, it provided me with a secure well paid job as a fully qualified radio technician. After paying most of my meagre civilian salary to grandad for board, I felt like I had won the lotto with free clothing, board and meals as well as medical and dental care thrown in.

Four years into my RAAF service I married Beverley, my wife of now fifty-four years. We started our early married life living in rented accommodation and later in RAAF housing. We began to think that maybe living in our own home would be a better more stable option for a married couple especially if we were to start a family. So, at the end of my enlistment in January 1973 I elected to be discharged in Melbourne. We purchased a block of land at

Chirnside Park where we built our first home. Our first child Benjamin now fifty years old at the time of writing, was born not long after we moved into our new home.

Once I had decided not to stay in the RAAF I became concerned as to whether or not my RAAF radio training would be accepted in the civilian world. I needn't have worried because I found that defence force trained technicians were highly sought after and I began my first civilian job as a computer systems engineer with Honeywell Pty Ltd immediately after being discharged. Honeywell later introduced call outs through the night so I and a few others joined Hewlett Packard in their computer service division.

During the time I worked at the RAAF 1TS (transmitting station) I had started to study for the Royal Society of Health Diploma for Public Health Inspectors Victoria. It was a three year diploma which I completed a year after being discharged from the RAAF. I decided to give health inspection a try, and was successful in obtaining a position with the Melbourne City Council. I was assigned to the Carlton area and spent quite some time inspecting various food establishments, apartment houses and Italian pizza restaurants in Lygon Street and surrounds. Later still after we moved into our new home at Chirnside Park, I took a position with the Ringwood City Council which meant a fifteen minute drive to work instead of the one and a half hour journey by train and tram to the Melbourne City Council Health Office.

After the thrill of working in a totally different career environment wore off, once again work seemed to become a mundane chore and the next few years I remember as the restless years as I tried out several different occupations, finishing up as a Technical Sales Representative with Canon Australia. My next career change though was the biggest and to many the strangest of all. I had been rather successful at Canon who had sent my wife and I on an South East Asia holiday to Penang and Singapore followed the next year by a South Pacific cruise as a way of them saying thanks for my sales contribution. It therefore came as quite a surprise to the sales manager when I told him that I was resigning to enter ordained ministry in the Anglican Church of Australia. In fact, it came as such a shock to him he almost fell backwards out of his office chair!

But that's what happened and I was ordained in St Paul's Cathedral, Melbourne firstly as a Deacon in 1984 and the following year as a Priest. Finally I had found the place where I believe God wanted me to be. Over the next thirty plus years, I served in a wide range of capacities as a Parish Priest, Industrial Chaplain, Victoria Police Chaplain, Defence Force Chaplain and for the last ten years of my working life as a Hospital Chaplain at the Prince Charles Hospital in Brisbane.

My retirement took place in 2015 at the age of sixty seven years, following which Bev and I spent a number of enjoyable holidays travelling in Europe, Canada, United States of America and New Zealand. As I write this our three children, Benjamin, Susanne and Meagan are all now middle aged and settled in their own homes, and Bev and I are the proud grandparents of six grandchildren ranging in age from eighteen months to twenty two years.

When I look back to the early years of my childhood and think of all that has taken place over almost seventy six years of life, I can only marvel at God's steadfast love and provision.

Truly, as the Good Book says, "My times are in your hands" (Ps 31:15).

www.ingramcontent.com/pod-product-compliance
Lightning Source LLC
Chambersburg PA
CBHW072015290426
44109CB00018B/2246